Brightlingsea
in old picture postcards

by A.L. Wakeling

European Library ZALTBOMMEL / THE NETHERLANDS

Mr. Alfred Wakeling, who has compiled this collecton of old Brightlingsea postcards and photographs, is the Community Council of Essex Recorder for Brightlingsea under that Council's local history recorder scheme. He is also the Assistant Keeper of the Records for the Cinque Port Liberty of Brightlingsea, secretary of the Brightlingsea Deputy's Christmas Gifts Fund and secretary of the Gild of Brightlingsea Freemen. From 1958 to 1965 Mr. Wakeling was the local newspaper correspondent for the 'East Essex Gazette'.

GB ISBN 90 288 2520 7

© 1983 European Library – Zaltbommel/The Netherlands

Fourth edition, 1996: reprint of the original edition of 1983.

INTRODUCTION

Brightlingsea, Essex, has the distinction of being the only connection with the Cinque Ports outside of Kent and Sussex. A Limb of Sandwich, the town does not appear in any of the early existing documents of the Ports nor in the Domesday survey of the Ports in 1229. However, it is known that Brightlingsea asked for and obtained a charter of confirmation in 1442, a part of which reads: *Be it remembered that on the 24th. day of July in the 20th year (1442) of the reign of King Henry VI of England after the Conquest at the Brodhull it was agreed that all the Residents and Inhabitants of the town of Brightlingsea in the County of Essex, which town from ancient times has been a member of the Cinque Ports and that the town of Sandwich make them a record of the same under the seal of office of mayorality there...*

There are two approaches to Brightlingsea, one by road and one by sea. The town is ten miles south-east of Colchester, the oldest recorded town in England, eleven miles north-west of Clacton and twenty-two miles south-west of Harwich — the gate to the continent of Europe. From the sea Brightlingsea is found on the north bank of a little creek which runs eastward from the River Colne. From 1866 the town was served well by trains until 1964 when the branch line from Wivenhoe was closed.

Brightlingsea's principal industry during the eighteenth and nineteenth centuries, and perhaps into relative recent times, was undoubtedly oyster dredging. But the severe winter of 1962/63 almost killed off this livelihood — the death knell being sounded with the closure of the Colne Oyster Fishery in May, 1963. And with its going Brightlingsea's identity as an oyster-town was lost. Stowboating for sprats also occupied the maritime fraternity and the little fish provided employment ashore for both men and women.

Brightlingsea began her long and successful connection with yachting in the 1840's. Many sailors crewed the racing and cruising yachts in the summer months and went fishing, scalloping and oyster-dredging at other times. The smacksmen, used to handling the cutter-rigged smacks, took naturally to fore-and-aft-rigged yachts. They also had a wide knowledge of the Thames estuary, the Channel and nearby waters. The creeks made good mud berths for laying-up the yachts and there were shipyards with skilled men for building and repairs. Brightlingsea became a naval base during World War One, and the shipyards were busy with Admiralty work, as they were again in World War Two.

Farming, mainly grain production, but with livestock on the reclaimed marshes, remained a substantial livelihood in the nineteenth and early twentieth centuries, but it was a boom in fishing that gave Brightlingsea its precarious added prosperity. Brightlingsea men still go to sea today, in the Royal and Merchant navies, also Customs and pilot services. And the much reduced local fishing and oyster enterprises provide employment for a hardy few.

An annual ceremony which is unique to Brightlingsea is Mayor-making on the first Monday following St. Andrew's Day each December when new inhabitants are also recognised and proclaimed Freemen. Residence in Brightlingsea for a year and a day is the new inhabitant's only necessary qualification and those of Brightlingsea birth, or 'who had the good sense to have married a Brightlingsea woman' are given their Freedom without payment. 'Foreigners' are fined eleven pence for the privilege. The Mayor-Deputy is chosen by the Freemen from three reputable inhabitants and, on being elected, now serves the town as its social head and as the Mayor of Sandwich's representative locally for the ensuing twelve months. In times past, with his six Assistants, who are also elected each year with him, the Deputy was responsible for the citizens' conduct, the Assistants particularly swearing to aid him in seeing that disorderly and unruly persons are punished and reformed 'that good order and good quiet may be ratified and established'. The Manor Court from earliest times managed the affairs of the town and later the Deputy and Assistants, with a certain amount of supervision by Sandwich, helped more especially in affairs outside the Court's scope. When these jurisdictions declined, the Vestry managed local affairs until the Local Government Act of 1888. Under that Act a Parish Council was formed and this lasted until an Urban District Council took over, with wider powers, nine years later. The present Town Council was born out of the reorganisation of local government on 1 April, 1974, which did away with the old Urban District Council and transferred almost all power to a new Tendring District Council in which Brightlingsea has but four votes out of a total of sixty. Effectively the new legislation took away all meaning of the word 'local' from local government. Notwithstanding the dilution of their powers the local town councillors exercised their prerogative of annually electing a Town Mayor from among their number instead of the traditional chairman. Thus Brightlingsea is in the unique position of having two Mayors. But, happily, the town has been able to accept this, seeing one as the civic head and the other as the social head.

The present Parish Church of All Saints, 'the mariners' church on the hill', has stood at the entrance to the town for some seven hundred years. Earlier buildings on the site are thought to date back to the coming of Christianity to Essex in 653. In 1969 the condition of the fabric had deteriorated to the point where it seemed likely that the church would be made redundant and closed. However, a body of 'Friends' was formed in the town to shoulder the responsibility of raising the funds needed to restore and maintain the church. As a result of their efforts interest in the church has been aroused and so far the necessary funds have been found.

A book of this nature is not possible without the inheritance left the author by many local photographers and historians, not least of all that master with the camera, Douglas Went and the man whose scholarship is the basis of much local knowledge, Doctor Edward Percival Dickin. To these two and the others must be extended a grateful acknowledgement.

Brightlingsea - February, 1983   A.L. Wakeling

1. Street Green, Brightlingsea, in 1880. Variously known as a part of Lower Green and of High Street in the 1890's before finally settling for Victoria Place to commemorate Queen Victoria's Diamond Jubilee in 1897. The buildings, on Barker's Farm, left and centre, were demolished in 1900 when Ladysmith Avenue was constructed and linked with Victoria Place. Here Mr. Abraham Pudney also had his greengrocery business. The King's Head public house (right) was originally a private house and a shop known as Wisbiche's.

PARISH CHURCH (EXTERIOR)

2. All Saints' Church, Brightlingsea, shortly after the restoration of the tower in 1886. Two years earlier the Essex earthquake hurled a pinnacle through the roof of the nave and this now stands in the church. The tower was restored at the expense of Mr. F.C. Capel, of Wilmington, Kent, in memory of his father, Mr. J.B. Capel, of North Cray, Bexley. In the bell-chamber there remains the bellframe and one of the mediaeval bells cast circa 1400 and inscribed 'Dulcis Sisto Melis Vocor Campana Michaelis' (I am sweet as honey and am called the bell Michael). There is also a small seventeenth century bell alongside. A trigonometrical point on the tower roof is used for the Ordinance Survey. The present church dates from about 1250, but had several predecessors, stretching back to the coming of Christianity to Essex in 653. The appointment of the first recorded incumbent was in 1237.

3. In 1904 Brightlingsea aquired a new railway station which was to last the life of the local line. Its demise, in 1964, was part of a country-wide system of line closures orchestrated by the then Chairman of the British Railways Board, Doctor Richard Beeching. The original station was a dismal, draughty, barnlike structure beloved of nobody. On New Year's Eve, 1901, merry-making crowds ceased their festivities on receiving the news 'the station's afire'. A large crowd gathered at the station and instead of watching silently and in awe, showed their delight by singing 'Auld Lang Syne' as it burnt down. The railway had come to Brightlingsea by way of a branch from Wivenhoe in 1866.

4. Among the early inns at Brightlingsea was the Ship with a mention in manor court rolls of 1666. It was one of only five local inns listed at Sandwich in 1805. By 1900 the number of inns in Brightlingsea had grown to twenty-four. But, by 1936, a third of this number, including the Ship, had their licences extinguished. When the Ship was demolished in 1978, it had been the home of Mr. John Osborne, the proprietor of Norfolk's Garage. During the 1914-1918 War, Australian engineers were billeted at the Ship inn and in an inscribed testimonial to Mr. Albert Norfolk, the host, on their returning home they described the Ship as 'No. 9 Victoria Place, the champion billet and the cure for all ills'.

Queen Street, Brightlingsea.

5. The Brightlingsea Society of the New Church moved into Queen Street in 1868 on the building of its new premises there. Based on the teachings of Emanuel Swedenborg, the Church's doctrines were introduced locally by Doctor Moses Fletcher in 1809, a recent arrival in the town to practice as a surgeon. The cost of the Queen Street church, shown here in a photograph taken in 1902, was £1,300. The iron railings fronting the church and adjoining school hall were removed as salvage during World War One and were not replaced. Son of a Lutheran Bishop and a member of the Swedish House of Nobles, Emanuel Swedenborg was an inventor, a scientist of the highest reputation and an author of standard works on metallurgy and mining, before immersing himself wholly into spiritual studies. Queen Street was formerly Spring Road, until 1887.

6. Jacobe's Hall after its restoration by Mr. Henry Havelock in 1919. The main structure of this most picturesque building in Brightlingsea's High Street, goes back to the thirteenth century. It is built on the half-H plan with a hall in the middle and cross wings at the east and west ends and is timber-framed in oak. Jacobe's was originally of one storey and the great hall had a hearth or brazier of fire on the floor, the smoke escaping through a louvred lantern in the roof. The central tie-beam and the base of the king-post are moulded. The exact date when the building became two-storied is unknown, but is thought to be sometime in the early part of the fifteenth century when owned by the Beriffe family. It was at this time that to save taking up space in the main hall by putting in an inside stairway the unique exterior brick turret stairway was built. A feature of Mr. Havelock's renovation was the removal of the shop which, in 1895, had been erected between the two cross wings which blocked off a beautiful doorway and part of the turret stairway.

7. Erected in 1835, St. James's Chapel-of-Ease was consecrated by the Bishop of London, the Right Reverend Charles James Blomfield who, during his episcopate from 1828 to his resignation in 1856 because of paralysis, saw some two hundred new churches consecrated in London, mainly through his efforts. Constructed with white bricks, the Chapel is of early English character. The western elevation is extremely picturesque and characteristic. The tower is placed at the south-west angle of the building and contains a staircase to the gallery. The principal entrance door is on the west side of the tower. The Chapel is crowned by a graceful spire. To commemorate Queen Victoria's Golden Jubilee of 1887, a public clock, known locally as 'the dial', was installed above the two lancet windows. Made by Gillet and Bland, of Croydon, the contract price was £125. This included a bell of four hundredweight for striking the hours and apparatus for illuminating the two dials.

TOWER STREET. BRIGHTLINGSEA. Nº 72

8. In 1883, eighteen years after the organisation had emerged from the Christian Mission in the East End of London, the Salvation Army came to Brightlingsea. Initially it operated from a wooden structure at Hurst Green before moving to Tower Street. Although the Army citadel had become well established on the Tower Street site, it was some thirty years, in 1932, before the present building, shown in the centre of the picture, was eventually purchased. To the present day, with trumpets and drum sounding and standard flying, army bands over the years have marched down Tower Street to Brightlingsea Hard and 'open air witness' there. Tower Street was also the scene of a wilful murder and suicide with the killing of Florence Booth, and the taking of his own life, by her husband Junius Booth. This was in rented furnished apartments at number 19, on December 6, 1912. The couple had established and run the Tower Cinema Theatre in Tower Street for the past three months or so. Junius Booth was the eldest of four sons born to Agnes Perry, the third wife of Junius Booth II, whose brother, John Wilkes Booth, is remembered as the assassin of President Abraham Lincoln, at Ford's Theatre, Washington.

9. On 26 December, 1912, the Empire Theatre opened in Station Road, Brightlingsea. With Mr. Harry Carr as General Manager, its full title was 'The Empire Theatre of Pictures and Varieties'. With an entire change of pictures every Monday and Thursday, screenings were given nightly at 8 p.m., with a Saturday matinee at 3 p.m. Prices of admission were 3d. Front seats, 4d. Cane seating, 6d. Tip-ups, 9d. Plush tip-ups. A change of name, to the Regal Cinema, came about early in 1938. In December, 1964, the Regal Cinema closed for the last time as a place of public entertainment having been sold to the electronics firm of Ormandy and Stollery Limited. And soon the carpenters arrived to transform the premises into workshops and offices.

10. On either side of 1900 sailmaking and shipchandlery dominated Brightlingsea's Waterside. Blyth Bros., E.A. Hibbs and Son, W.F. Pattison, Pannell and Hibbs, John R. Foot, A.W. Went are six prominent firms that served a very large yachting station, which Brightlingsea had become, with upwards of one hundred yachts being laid-up locally in winter quarters. Waterside was also the home of Bridges and Son, blockmakers, and the yachtbuilders Albert Aldous, Robert Aldous, John James and Douglas Stone.

11. Number 39 New Street, Brightlingsea, in 1910, the haircutting and shaving saloon of Mr. William Wesley Folkard. In addition to his barber's duties, Mr. Folkard was the local Registrar of Marriages and the Assessor and Income tax collector. At number 47 was the Freemasons Tavern, proprietor Robert O. Barnard, now a private residence.

12. New Street, Brightlingsea, in 1901. Dominating this main thoroughfare from the town centre to the waterside is the Royal Hotel, which was opened just four years previously. Up to 1860 New Street was known as Waterside and was the linking road between the Hard and the Street, now Victoria Place and High Street.

Ladysmith Avenue, Brightlingsea.

13. Ladysmith Avenue, a residential thoroughfare developed at the turn of the century. Named after the town in Natal, South Africa, in which a number of Brightlingsea men served during the Boer War. Between the two World Wars and afterwards Ladysmith Avenue was the home of the Primitive Methodist Church, known locally as 'the Gooseberry Chapel' because of a practice of selling gooseberries there to raise church funds, but now demolished. Here was also the Mineral Water Works operated by Mr. F. Cracknell whose bottles, with their 'glarny' method of sealing, are still found and cherished by young people locally. Brightlingsea's Police Station has also been in Ladysmith Avenue since 1902. 'The Rammekens' (right), one-time residence of John Angier, master mariner, was named by him to recall his many visits to the Dutch anchorage of that name off Flushing.

ANCHOR HOTEL. BRIGHTLINGSEA. PROPRIETAR E. PERCIVAL.

14. The new Anchor Hotel on the waterfront at Brightlingsea was opened in 1903 with Mr. Ernest Percival as Proprietor. This handsome house, built in the timbered style, replaced a weather-boarded building licenced as an inn in 1805.

15. The Hard, Brightlingsea, where one fearful day in March, 1883, large numbers of people gathered in vain for news of missing husbands, fathers and sons. Some stood in groups or paced imaginary deck's lengths, in spite of the cutting snow squalls. Some mounted the various accessible elevations, telescope in hand. All were awaiting the return of three of Brightlingsea's fishing fleet, the 'Recruit', the 'Conquest' and the Yarmouth lugger 'Mascotte', from the Terschelling oyster-grounds in the North Sea. But furious gales had done their worse and of the three ill-fated vessels not the least of traces has been since discovered. Nineteen men perished in the disaster, involving nineteen families with thirty-two children fatherless. In happier times the Hard is a colourful scene as both the professional and amateur mariner tends his craft for livelihood or recreation. For the Reverend Arthur Pertwee, Vicar of Brightlingsea, it was the venue for his monthly jottings 'Gossip from the Hard' from 1882-1917.

SPLASH POINT, BRIGHTLINGSEA.

16. Standing offshore by Splash Point is Bateman's Tower, a bathing hut built for Mr. John Bateman, seven times Brightlingsea's Mayor-Deputy. Erected in 1882, the Tower retained its conical cap until 1940 when the local Royal Observer Corps removed it to facilitate the spotting of enemy aircraft. The Tower is said to be a fine example of the 'modern' use of Roman cement. It is now used as a starting hut for sailing races in the River Colne and Creekmouth organised by the Colne Yacht Club. The photograph, taken in July, 1932, just after the official opening of the West Marsh Pleasure Grounds, shows part of the concrete wall of over half a mile in length starting from near Waterside and finishing at Bateman's Tower.

17. The early 1920's at All Saints' Church where the Lych-gate in memory of Canon Arthur Pertwee, Vicar of Brightlingsea, from 1872 to 1917, had recently been dedicated by Canon Tollington, the Rural Dean. The Cinque Port coat of arms may be seen engraved on the structure. Canon Pertwee was deeply interested in the welfare of seafaring men. Even in his old age he climbed the tower of All Saints' to give lantern light to the fishing fleet entering the harbour. He devoted himself to the care of the sick and the poor. A cross which marks his grave in All Saints' churchyard is inscribed 'He walked with God'.

18. In January, 1887, Brightlingsea gained a new hotel — the Royal. Built for Mr. Fred Miller, Brewer, the Royal Hotel offered 'every home comfort, good stabling, a lock-up coach house and a porter who attended every train'. The proprietor, Mr. G. Ash, was also able to arrange guns and boats for local wildfowling. The Royal ceased to be a hotel in 1950.

Coastguard Station, Brightlingsea.

19. Brightlingsea Coastguard Station in Backwaterside Lane, off Brightlingsea High Street. Here, in addition to homes for the coastguards, an armoury was established. The coastguard service at the latter end of the nineteenth century provided, as the name indicates, protection of the coast against invasion from the sea. Assistance was also given in shipwrecks and the members played a large part in the prevention of smuggling on a large scale. They also helped in the training of the local Royal Naval Reserve which operated at the Battery Station on St. Osyth Stone. At the outbreak of the 1914-1918 War the coastguard personnel were called up for duty and on the cessation of hostilities the station closed. The row of houses are now dwellings for retired Salvation Army officers. In earlier days the coastguards were accommodated in the cottages in Sydney Street, opposite the gasworks.

The Creek, Brightlingsea.

20. Night is falling over Brightlingsea Creek and the ferrymen's boats, tethered to the Causeway and each other, are at rest. But while there are passengers about there are ferrymen to row them 'over the other side' – to St. Osyth Stone and East Mersea shore.

MARTELLO TOWER AND COASTGUARD STATION, BRIGHTLINGSEA.

21. Work on a Royal Naval Reserve Station on St. Osyth Stone commenced in June, 1891, and continued throughout the following year and into 1893. Initially the Battery mounted a single gun weighing six and a half tons which was taken to its site by road from Brightlingsea rail station when plans to float it across the creek proved unfeasible. A 4.7 gun was added in 1900. In March, 1906, the Station was closed, a decision having been made to train the Reservists afloat only. A farewell exhibition and entertainment, given by R.N.R. men and friends, was well attended, the resultant profits being divided between the Merchant Seamen's Orphanage and the Essex and Colchester hospital. The adjacent Martello Tower was built in 1808.

22. Thursday and the shop is shut for 'early closing'. From 1894 to 1903 the general stores at 125 Tower Street, Brightlingsea, was the livelihood of Miss Sarah Jane Root. The ladder against the front of Southern Cross Villas pre-supposes the workmen have gone off to lunch. And Tower Street at the turn of the century quietly slumbers in the afternoon sunshine.

23. Station Road, Brightlingsea. The terrace of six cottages here, each with its individual front garden, was known locally as Sparrow Row. These dwellings no longer exist having been replaced with a single-block tenement appropriately named Sparrow House. Its neighbour (left) is the Railway Hotel. The adjacent cottages and out buildings were demolished in 1912, the land becoming the site of the new Empire Theatre. Nearby, leading to Brightlingsea's railway station, was Gandergoose Green.

Victoria Place, Brightlingsea

Copyright Series by Leverett, Brightlingsea

24. Victoria Place, Brightlingsea, before the building of the Post Office on the corner of Queen Street in 1905. The building at the centre of the picture is the New Church schoolroom, erected in 1876.

25. The early morning sun casts shadows in pre-World War One Sydney Street, Brightlingsea, as Postman George Trubshoe makes the day's first mail deliveries. At number 104 Arthur Eade is baking the day's bread continuing the daily practice of his predecessor Albert John Pearmain.

26. The Swan Hotel, in Brightlingsea's High Street, built late in the sixteenth century. With cross-wings at the east and west ends, there is a seventeenth century addition on the north side. Inside the building are some original moulded beams. This view was taken in 1905, just after the house had been completely renovated.

Hurst Green. Brightlingsea.

27. Hurst Green, Brightlingsea. The derivation of Hurst is said locally to be hearse, from its triangular shape. It may be noted that the English archers at Crecy were drawn-up in the form of a 'hearse' i.e. in a triangular formation. Hurst Green seems not to have suffered much from encroachment over the years though in more recent times some land has been taken from it on the west side and at the south west corner. For many years, before the coming of the Recreation Ground, Hurst Green was the venue for local football matches. And a baseball match between teams from the USA cruiser 'Chattanooga' then lying in the Colne, was staged at Hurst Green in 1919. In 1739 a Dancing Master owned and lived in a cottage called Chickens or the Chicken House on the west side of Hurst Green — now numbers 11, 12 and 13.

Church Hill, Brightlingsea

Copyright Series by Leverett, Brightlingsea

28. The road into Brightlingsea climbing Church Hill circa 1905. Ahead looms the Parish Church of All Saints — the 'mariners church on the hill'.

Blest Landmark to the sailor homeward bound, / Dear sign of home, where love and joy are found; / How sweet to think that safely o'er the sea / His vessel once again in port shall be; / How sweet to think that once again his step / Shall pass his threshold, and with lip to lip, / His greetings cheer the lonely waiting heart, / From whose embrace, he found it hard to part.

Thy tow'ring form from age to age has wrought, / The peaceful joy that many a heart has sought; / Years have rolled on in centuries o'er thy head, / Unchanged alone thou art amid the dead. / Beneath thy quiet shadows lie at rest, / Those, who wave-toss'd thro' life, thy form have blest.

Thy massive height, how like those truths sublime, / That 'neath thy walls have rung from far-gone time; / Severe, yet lovely, — old, yet ever new, / Peacegiving and all beautiful to view.

A.E.R. — 1875.

29. Tuesday, November 12, 1918, and Brightlingsea celebrates the signing of the Armistice the previous day with services at All Saints' Church. The Procession in the afternoon was one vast pilgrimage to the Parish Church and so large was the congregation there that those who could not get into the building joined in a great 'overflow' service outside. Leading the Procession were mounted Australian engineers from their Brightlingsea Training Depot.

30. Despite the quiet appearance of Brightlingsea's High Street circa 1905, Mrs. Julia Rawcliffe's Drapery and Millinery shop on the corner with John Street (late Hog Lane) is open for business. Next door at Albert Seaman's boot and shoe shop a customer has left his bicycle against the shopfront while making a purchase. Ted Eade's baker's cart awaits the evening's bread in the road.

31. No sooner than the camera appears then out come the onlookers in Brightlingsea's High Street about 1905. Edward Henry Eade, baker, moved his business into High Street, from Wellington Street, in 1893.

High Street, Brightlingsea.

32. A distinguished trio in Brightlingsea's High Street circa 1910. At number 47, Mr. George Angier, tailor; at number 51, Dr. Edward Percival Dickin, physician and medical officer of health to the Urban District Council; and at number 53, Mr. Albert Aldous Jefferies, oyster merchant and Lloyds Agent. Opposite, the original entrance to Jacobe's Hall is blocked-in by Mr. George W. Crane's fruiters and confectionery shop.

33. The village Blacksmith, Victoria Place, Brightlingsea, in 1895. Demolished in 1910, the smithy served the local community for many years and, at the time of this photograph, was worked by Jesse Hill junior. Meantime, his father, Jesse Hill senior, operated the smithy in Church Road. Up to 1897 that part of Victoria Place in which the young Jesse's premises were sited was part of High Street. Next door was T.R. Mills, Clothier, Hatter and Outfitter to the local men —about— town.

OYSTER PITS, BRIGHTLINGSEA

34. Now seemingly abandoned waste land, in some instances as receptacles for household rubbish, Brightlingsea's oyster pits once played an important part in the local enterprise. Here were stored the oysters previously dredged from the Colne or the special fattening-grounds of the Pyefleet, to await customers' orders and despatch elsewhere.

35. Ranks of yachts laid up in their winter quarters along Easterly, in 1930. The 1920's and 1930's were the times when hundreds of Brightlingsea men went to sea, and yachting was a great local industry. And when the yards of Douglas Stone, John James and Robert Aldous, and the Syndicate mud berths, the Stage, Emanuel Griggs' ground, and the Cook Brothers', Wenlock Brothers' and E.A. Hibbs' mud berths were a forest of masts. From Fieldgate's Dock to the Ropewalk, the yachts at rest swayed like growing wheat. Shown, left to right: S.Y. 'Elsie', S.Y. 'Vanda', M.Y. 'Anne Marie', Sch. 'Tamesis', M.Y. 'Endymion', S.Y. 'Karen', S.Y. 'Titania', S.Y. 'Bronwen', S.Y. 'Strathspey', S.Y. 'Elfreda' and Sch. 'Grey Goose'.

36. A Whippet tank, which had been secured for the occasion by Commander R. Hartland Mahon RN, was the centre of interest in the street procession which was the highlight of Brightlingsea's Peace Celebrations on July 19, 1919. Over four thousand flags, many bearing the arms of the Cinque Ports, decorated the town which was en-fete for the long-awaited celebrations. A programme of sports was carried out on Mr. Keeble's meadow near the railway station in the afternoon during which the Salvation Army band and the town band played selections of music. In the evening there was a fancy dress carnival, a procession through the principle streets and a bon-fire on West Marsh with rockets.

37. Members of the Naval Base were responsible for the construction of HMS 'Brightlingsea', a model battleship, which lead the procession on July 19, 1919, during the town's Peace Celebrations. Next day the men of the Base entertained local children to tea on St. Osyth Stone. Transported to the Stone by motor launches, the children and accompanying adults enjoyed 'all the fun of the fair' until darkness brought proceedings to a close. While the young people were the guests of the Navy, over three hundred adults, including discharged, demobilised and serving soldiers and sailors were the guests at a 'free and easy' evening in the Empire Theatre by invitation of Mr. Thomas Bartlett Howard. As part of the local Peace Celebrations, the President of the Workmen's Institute (to be known after the event as the Thomas Howard Institute) was handed deeds of the freehold house and premises of 22 Upper Park Road and a piece of land near the waterworks for use as a rifle-range. In an earlier life 22 Upper Park Road was the White Horse Inn.

38. Heroney Wood, Brightlingsea, the home of the heron. Situated on the road linking the twin manors of Brightlingsea and Moverons, Heroney Wood is also known locally as Thicks Wood.

39. Having been closed for almost six years, Brightlingsea's Bayard Recreation Ground was re-opened to the public on April 7, 1921. Present to formally declare the 'Rec' open was Councillor W.R. Seabrooke, chairman of Brightlingsea Urban District Council. The First World War was in its infancy when the military authorities requisitioned the local recreation ground for use as a drill ground and later for a tented camp. And two years were needed after the cessation of hostilities to make the playing areas fit for sports again. The need for a home for both football and cricket in Brightlingsea was appreciated during the late 1880's by a small band of sporting enthusiasts. Meantime the periodical contests at both games continued on Hurst Green and elsewhere locally. Then came the news, in November 1890 that an approach for financial help to Mr. M. Bayard Brown, an American millionaire, who had made his home in the River Colne aboard his yacht 'Valfreyia', had proved successful. This help was in the form of a promised £250 donation towards the provision of a recreation ground, later to be increased, in May, 1891, to £600 which met the purchase price of a field of six acres and three rods with £50 to spare. A further donation of £100 from Mr. Bayard Brown covered the cost of planting and turfing the ground. As a compliment to the nationality of Brightlingsea's generous benefactor, July 4, 1893, was chosen as 'opening day'. In 1897 the custody of the Bayard Recreation Ground was transferred to the Brightlingsea Urban District Council.

40. The Deputy and Lady Deputy of the Cinque Port Liberty of Brightlingsea, Mr. and Mrs. Thomas Bartlett Howard, with collectors on Geranium Day, 1929. On this special day each year street and door-to-door collections are made in aid of the National Institute for the Blind. The picture shows the group assembled at Brightlingsea's War Memorial in Victoria Place.

41. Providing frequent services from Brightlingsea to Clacton, Walton and Harwich, from 1919, was a fleet of Silver Queen motor omnibusses. This 'double decker' is seen in Victoria Place completing a journey from Clacton in the summer of 1919.

42. A Silver Queen char-a-banc at Clacton prior to returning to Brightlingsea in the 1920's. The maximum permitted speed of these vehicles was twelve miles per hour.

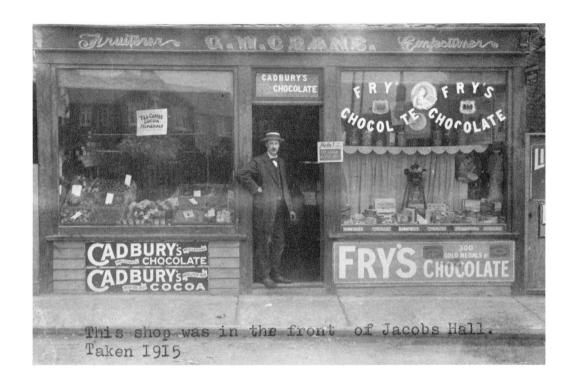

43. Mr. H.E. Phillips at the door of his shop fronting Jacobe's Hall in 1915. Mr. Phillips took over the business of G.W. Crane in September, 1914. He moved into his own premises, next door, in 1919, when Crane's shop was removed during Mr. Henry Havelock's restoration of Jacobe's Hall.

44. Brightlingsea Fire Brigade, in 1911, was under the control of Brightlingsea Urban District Council with its Clerk, Mr. W.I. Osborn, as Captain. His Lieutenant was Mr. A.F. Whislay, an engineer and metal worker in the town whose business at Waterside was established in 1873. The Firemen were Messrs. H.V. Lord, J. Dines, F. Bell, R. Cooper, A.E. Mann, W. Copsey, H. Copsey, J. Osborn, A. Austin, H. Barr, E. Angier and H. Fenn. In the event of a fire a person calling a fireman and obtaining his ticket was paid sixpence on delivering the ticket to the Captain. A person giving a Brigade call on the first alarm at the Forrester's Hall was paid five shillings. To do this the glass in the alarm box was broken and the handle turned until a Fireman arrived.

High Street, Brightlingsea

45. High Street, Brightlingsea, from Victoria Place, circa 1900. The town's principal thoroughfare, High Street, in 1897, lost its late Street Green area which became Victoria Place. Up to the coming of Ladysmith Avenue, in 1900, the way to Brightlingsea's Hard, by road, was via Church Road, Spring Road (a part of which is now Queen Street), The Street (now Victoria Place after a spell as High Street) and Waterside (now New Street for most of its length). Awaiting the afternoon's customers in our picture are the drapers Joseph H. Barnes at numbers 52 and 53, Joseph Bagley, tailor and outfitter, at 54 and the International Stores at 55.

43920. BRIGHTLINGSEA. HIGH STREET.

46. Despite being captioned Brightlingsea High Street this view is mainly of Victoria Place in 1905, with High Street beyond St. James's Chapel-of-Ease, centre. Today it is the site of Brightlingsea's War Memorial.

47. The 'Swan Deeps' circa 1905, that part of Victoria Place and High Street to which gathered each evening Brightlingsea's mariners seeking berths in the ocean-racing yachts. Opposite, on the corner of New Street, stands the imposing premises of John Field and Son, Grocers and Drapers, who were also the proprietors of the Hurst Green Stores.

VICTORIA HOUSE.

48. Fred Went, stationer, bookseller, printer, bookbinder, advertising, insurance and news agent, established his business in 1887 on the corner of High Street and Tower Street, Brightlingsea. And in keeping with the times his premises were given the name Victoria House. Publisher and founder of the Brightlingsea Almanack, Advertiser, Tide and Time Table and Visitor's Guide Book, Mr. Went's shop was a veritable Aladdin's Cave of commodities. In addition to supplying daily and weekly newspapers, birthday, wedding and memorial cards and booklets, he retailed all kinds of tobacco and cigars, as well as pouches, pipes, knives, walking-sticks, work-boxes, writing-desks and artists' materials, tennis and seaside requisites. Mr. Went's proclamations announced that yacht and ship orders were promptly executed and schools, clubs and 'the trade' supplied.

49. Always at the mercy of gluts and shortages, Brightlingsea's inshore fishermen between the wars gleaned a variable living stowboating. This method of fishing, where the anchored vessels rides head to tide, with its open-jawed net fastened from partway down the anchor cable, trapped the shoals of sprats as they were driven-in by the tide. Spratting was indeed a precarious livelihood. A bad season might bring a smack only a few shillingsworth of fish. A glut would send prices plunging, because of the very restricted two-month season, and the fish would have to be sold off cheaply as manure. A sprat harvest once ashore was handled by a number of outlets, including local smoke-houses and six pickling yards, one in Colne Road, one in Duke Street, two in Tower Street, one in the yard of the 'Duke of Wellington' inn and one in the yard of the 'Freemasons Tavern'. This picture was taken outside one of the yards in December, 1912.

50. A large number of people's livings depended upon the winter sprat fishery. Not least of all in the local pickling yards where work would be in full swing around Christmas. The processed sprats were put into barrels for export to the Continent, the Scandinavian countries and to Russia being sent there from Brightlingsea rail station via Colchester and Harwich.

51. Preparing the sprats for smoking at Musson and Company's fishyard, Brightlingsea. After being washed in fresh water, laid in salt for six or seven hours and fresh-water rinsed, the fish were skewered onto metal spits. Then they were wind-dried for a few hours prior to being placed in smoke from oak chippings damped down with oak sawdust. Brightlingsea's smoked sprats were a delicacy par excellence.

52. A familiar sight in Brightlingsea's Victoria Place until it was demolished in 1978 was the white-washed, single-storey building which, for the last forty years of its existence, was used as the 'front office' for A.W. Norfolk and Son's garage and motor repair business. On his return from serving in HM forces during World War One, Mr. William Bunting opened-up there as a butcher being succeeded at his death by Mr. Ralph Durrell in 1922, when our photograph was taken. Previously it was used by Mr. James Carter as a fishshop. During Mr. Durrell's occupation, the premises became the first butchers in Brightlingsea to store and retail refrigerated meat.

53. While Brightlingsea was involved with the Peace Celebrations on July 19, 1919, a British North Sea Patrol Vessel, the NS7, passed overhead. Below is Hill House, Chapel Road.

54. Charles Christmas Trubshoe, born January 28, 1824, died July 11, 1889, Brightlingsea's first policeman. The practice of appointing residents in turn to act as unpaid constables, in force for so many centuries, began to erode in the early 1800's. In 1832 the Tendring Magistrates wanted to appoint additional constables, but the parishioners objected as these appointments had always been made by the Court Leet. At length it was agreed that the Court Leet should appoint an additional six. At the next meeting of the Court a further eight constables were appointed and special Leets were held to swear them into office. However, it was enacted in 1842 that a Court Leet should not elect a petty constable except for purposes unconnected with the preservation of the peace. Born in Little Easton, near Dunmow, Charles Trubshoe joined the Police Force in June, 1845, and was posted to Brightlingsea where he served until retirement on June 30, 1884. Married to Rosina Franklin on May 18, 1847, Charles and his wife were blessed with four daughters, Rosina Mary, Emily, Laura and Julia, and two sons, William and George, all of whom were Brightlingsea born.

55. The earliest known Post Office in Brightlingsea was a small room added in front of 9 High Street. Later the office was moved to larger premises at 17 High Street. For some fifty years Brightlingsea's mail was in the charge of the family Minter, William from the 1850's to 1866, Rhoda 1867-1884 and Samuel 1884-1904 — latterly from premises on the corner of New Street and High Street. In 1905 Brightlingsea's Post Office removed to its present site in Victoria Place, on the corner of Queen Street. The first Postmaster there was Emile H.A. Haestier, who stayed until his transfer to Stanstead in 1912. He was succeeded by Rhoda Fuller, pictured here with her staff just after her appointment.

56. Dominating the Chancel at All Saints' Church is a most elaborate monument to Nicholas Magens, who is buried under a fine leger slab in front of the altar. A German merchant who made his home in London, Magens was a founding father of Lloyd's marine insurance. He bought the estates at Brightlingsea a year before his death. The monument in the rococo style was executed in marble by Nicolas Read, a pupil of Roubiliac, and erected in 1779. The central globe shows California as an island on the west coast of America. The angel of the Ressurection stands to the left holding a record of Magens' life and this is balanced by a huge cornucopia and finely carved anchor to the right. In 1848, at the age of eighty-seven, his son, Magens Dorrien Magens, Lord of the Manors of Brightlingsea and Moveron's since 1794, died.

INTERIOR OF PARISH CHURCH.

57. An interior view of All Saints' Church circa 1890. The stained glass of the fifteenth century window is Victorian, but of good quality. It has three cinquefoil lights. In the north aisle the painted glass showing St. Paul is Flemish of the sixteenth century. The organ was placed in the ancient south chapel during the last century. Memorial brasses remaining are to the Beriffe family.

58. A local Hunt meeting at the Hard during the early twenties. Traditionally the foxhounds were assembled at Hurst Green, but on the occasion of our photograph the Brightlingsea venue was changed to the Hard in front of the Anchor Hotel. Mine host, centre, was Mr. E. (Bob) Percival, seen accompanied by his daughter Elsie (Mrs. Clifford Gould). Providing an industrial and maritime backcloth are Mr. Summer's blacksmith shop and Mr. Jerry Vincent's oyster and sprat sheds.

THE BEACH, BRIGHTLINGSEA.

59. If the modern practice is to undress for the beach, in circa 1900 Brightlingsea it was the opposite. For the weekend excursion to St. Osyth Stone and the beach there the local trippers put on their Sunday best and 'got away from it all'!

that remain in the broad Sea

CHARLES BARBER	EDWARD NEALE	GEORGE KEMP	GEORGE PARMENGER	OSCAR SALMON	GEORGE EVERETT
AGED·23	AGED·24	AGED·21	AGED·16	AGED·26	AGED·34
lost·in·the·Smack	Native·of·Gt·Bromley	Native·of·Kirby·le·Soken	Native·of·Kirby·le·Soken	Master	lost·in·the·Lugger
Conquest	lost·in·the·Smack·Conquest	lost·in·the·Smack·Conquest	lost·in·the·Smack·Conquest	lost·in·the·Lugger·Mascotte	Mascotte
in·the·North·Sea	in·the·North·Sea	in·the·North·Sea	in·the·North·Sea	in·the·North·Sea	in·the·North·Sea
March·6·1883	March·6·1883	March·6·1883	March·6·1883	March·6·1883	March·6·1883

60. The idea of recording on tiles the deaths at sea of Brightlingsea seamen, occurred to the Reverend Arthur Pertwee in 1883 after the shocking disaster of March 6 of that year. Then, it will be recalled, nineteen Brightlingsea men were drowned off the Dutch coast. He worked back from records of the loss of life at sea to 1872, the year of his induction at Brightlingsea as Vicar. The Reverend Pertwee was helped in the work of recording these tragedies and installing the tiles by the churchwarden Mr. William Stammers, by Mr. Arthur Blyth, who 'wrote' the inscriptions, and by others of the parish. Mr. Stammers also bequeathed £200, the income from which should be used for the erection and maintenance of the tiles. As far as it is known, the frieze of memorial tiles at All Saints' Church is unique in English churches. Up to 1919, the year of the Reverend Pertwee's death, one hundred and seventy-seven tiles had been installed. By 1983, one hundred years since the old vicar first thought of instituting the custom, two hundred and twelve tiles comprised this simple but expressive memorial at the mariners' church on the hill.

By the Hard, Brightlingsea.

61. The 'Will Everard', fetched up on Brightlingsea's Hard, is the centre of attention by Sunday morning strollers in the early 1900's. Built by Fellows of Yarmouth for Everards of Greenhythe, to trade between British and Continental coasts, this 250 ton Thames Spritsail barge was a fine example of a type of vessel peculiar to the Suffolk, Essex and Kent coasts. Its shallow draught and flat bottom was ideally suited to the local conditions of a coast line dotted with sandbanks and with loading ports in shallow rivers and backwaters. Perhaps one of their greatest advantages lay in the simplicity of the spritsail rig used enabling a crew of only two men or, as in many a case, a man and his wife, to handle them; although the regular continental traders would carry two men and a boy. Many of these craft were built in Brightlingsea shipyards, owned by Brightlingsea merchants and sailed by Brightlingsea mariners. The sailing barge evolved during the early nineteenth century and reached its heyday between the 1870's and 1930's from which time, owing to its competition with more modern and faster steel-built diesel-engined craft, plus the competition from road transport, it gradually declined and finally went out of existence as commercial craft in the 1950's.

Brightlingsea Church from the Road.

62. All Saints' Church circa 1887. Visitors to Brightlingsea frequently ask why the parish church is so far from the town. It might be more apt to ask why the town is so far from the church since the town came into existence much later. Several reasons have been expressed over the years as to the position of the building; particularly as the church stands at the cross roads with Moverons and Thorington over which the local priest is said to have had jurisdiction. Moverons was of importance from earliest times and the Romans had an encampment there, also they used the ford to Alresford. But the popular and perhaps more practical reason for the church being away from the people is that at the time of the Black Death in 1349 what remained of the population fled to the waterside and there rebuilt. Then there is the suggestion that a high point was the obvious location on which to build a church.

63. A famous Brightlingsea mariner, Captain Edward Sycamore, skipper of 'Shamrock 2', the second of five unsuccessful challengers of that name for the America's Cup, used to meet a local farmer at the Swan Hotel. One day, in 1906, over drinks, they were discussing the skills of their respective callings. Eventually the captain challenged the farmer to a ploughing match, to prove that by using his compass he could plough a furrow as straight as the farmer could. The challenge was accepted, and, a Saturday afternoon being fixed for the contest, a large crowd assembled on the farmer's field. The betting was about even. The seaman won. When Sir Thomas Lipton, owner of the Shamrocks, heard about the contest he presented a cup to be competed for annually. When after some years horses on the farm were replaced by machinery, the matches were discontinued and the cup lodged in a local bank, where it stayed until it was given to Brightlingsea Sailing Club. It is now one of the many trophies and cups raced for under the club's burgee. Our picture postcard shows Captain Sycamore instructing a local beauty in the landlubbers' art.

Anchor Hotel and Shelter, Brightlingsea.

64. Brightlingsea's Shelter at the Hard, a gift to the town by the American millionaire, Mr. Bayard Brown, of the S.Y. 'Valfreyia'. In 1912, paid for by private donations and with the small balance of the Coronation Celebration Committee's fund, a Clock was erected on the south side of the Shelter as a permanent memorial of the coronation of H.M. King George V two years earlier.

Unveiling Brightlingsea War Memorial Oct. 20th. 1921.

65. Brightlingsea's memorial to the 1914-1918 War dead, in Victoria Place, was unveiled by Brigadier-General F.W. Towsey, CMG, CBE, DSO, on October 20, 1921. After the ceremony of unveiling and dedication a very large number of floral tributes was placed around the memorial. One of the wreaths was from the local schoolchildren and was carried by Winnie Dines, Donald Eade and Charles Westall, who had all lost their fathers in the war. It was fitting that the Reverend Arthur Francis Waskett, BA, as an ex-serviceman, should pronounce the actual words of dedication. Other clergy taking part were the Vicar, the Reverend R.F. Rendell, BA, FRAS, and the Reverends H. Deans (New Church) and W. Rosewarne (Congregational Church). Buglers of the 2nd. Leinster Regiment sounded the Last Post. Also attending the ceremony was Councillor G.C. Solley, who was making the first visit of a Mayor of Sandwich to Brightlingsea since Richard Parrett came here some three hundred years earlier during the reign of Queen Elizabeth I. Sandwich councillors, Aldermen Hicks and Stopes and Councillor Watts accompanied their Mayor. The Deputy of Brightlingsea, Mr. T.B. Howard, was also present.

66. Brightlingsea's War Memorial. Subscriptions totalling £1,050 were received in response to an Appeal initiated by the Reverend R. Fermor Rendell, Vicar, as early as March, 1918, to provide Brightlingsea with a permanent War Memorial. Sited in Victoria Place, the memorial is in grey granite, with two bronze pictorial panels and two tablets bearing one hundred and eight names of the fallen of World War One. It was designed by Captain R. Goulden, RE, who served in Brightlingsea with the Engineers during the war. A further twenty-three names were added to the memorial after World War Two.

67. Mr. McEvers Bayard Brown, 1852-1926. Born in Brooklyn, New York, Mr. Bayard Brown, as he later became universally known, first came to Brightlingsea to charter S.Y. 'Juno' in which to start yachting. In 1887 he purchased S.Y. 'Lady Torfrida', 623 tons, from Sir William Pearce, Bart., and cruised extensively in her. He then sold 'Lady Torfrida' to the Grand Duke Michael of Russia, a cousin of the Czar, and, in 1889, purchased, also from Sir William, the palatial steam yacht 'Valfreyia', 735 tons, the vessel which became his home for the rest of his life. Arriving in the River Colne on June 5, 1889, 'Valfreyia' dropped anchor a few hundred yards off Brightlingsea — to remain there for thirty-four years until removing, in 1923, to the Rennie Drydock at Wivenhoe. After Mr. Brown's death, in 1926, 'Valfreyia' was sold to the Jam of Narwanagar, generally known as Prince Ranji. Mr. Brown was a philanthropist to eccentricity, giving away large sums of money to scores of applicants who besieged him day and night. Practically every day, summer and winter, boats were ranged around the American millionaire's yacht; sometimes twenty or thirty boats containing some sixty or seventy people were assembled at one time. Brightlingsea has much to be grateful for to Mr. Brown. His gift of the Bayard Recreation Ground, donations towards the enlargement of the church school and improvements to the Hard plus the provision of the Hard Shelter were only some of the local projects receiving his generous benevolence. Following a memorial service in St. Mary's Parish Church, Wivenhoe, Mr. Brown's body was conveyed to London en-route to the United States for interment in the family vault at Brooklyn.

68. Any collection of Brightlingsea photographs would be incomplete without two nonengenarians of the 1930's. Born within three days of each other, in March, 1840, Thomas Rouse (left) and Charles Chaplin exemplified the sturdy breed of Brightlingsea men whose maritime calling took them worldwide. Both men started work at eight years of age, Mr. Rouse in looking after pigs, of which he was scared and left the first day, and Mr. Chaplin at rook scaring. Apprenticeships followed for both young men, Thomas to the salvage trade and Charles to the smack 'Arrow' on which he made trips to Jersey for oysters. He was with Mr. Thomas Hall for twenty-seven years, ten years aboard the illfated 'Mignonette' and then the yawl 'Gertrude'. Other boats in which he served were 'Danitza', of 110 tons, the 40-ton yawl 'Daisy' and the Duke of Somerset's 'Caprice'. He worked on the water until he retired at the age of eighty-four, the last four being spent ferrying. Mr. Rouse worked in the salvage boats until he was twenty-one. And, before retiring at eighty-two from a shore job in the Aldous shipyard, spent most of his time yachting in the summer and stowboating in the winter. He will be remembered locally as the cook/steward in the 'Venus', 'Gardinia', 'Advocet', 'Sybil' and the S.Y. 'Ratter'. The two life-long friends were finally parted in September, 1931, with the death of Mr. Chaplin which was followed by Mr. Rouse's demise in January, 1934.

69. Choosing Day in the Ringing-room at All Saints' Church, Brightlingsea, December 5, 1927. Except for a lapse of some eighty years from 1805, Brightlingsea has been electing Deputies to the Mayors of Sandwich since 1442 – and perhaps earlier! The annual Cinque Port ceremony also includes the recognition of new inhabitants and so large was the number of men present in 1927 that the proceedings were transferred to the green immediately before the Lychgate at the entrance to the churchyard. Chosen by his fellow Freemen as Deputy of the Cinque Port Liberty of Brightlingsea for 1927/28 was Mr. A.W. Norfolk from the traditional 'three reputable inhabitants'. At the same time his six Assistants were elected as were the Officers of the Liberty. Our picture shows the celebrated Dr. Edward Percival Dickin, Keeper of the Records, reading the minutes of the previous year's proceedings with the treasurer, Mr. Harry Chamberlain, on his left. In the chair is the retiring Deputy, Mr. Charles Brasted, with the senior Assistant, the Reverend F.A. Grosvenor Smyth, on his right. It was on this occasion that the Cinque Port Liberty Sports Shield was first presented for annual competition between local schools.

70. Brightlingsea Boy Scouts and Church Lads Brigade members were among the local youth who collected for the Titanic Widows and Orphans Relief Fund during April, 1912. As a result of ss 'Titanic' sinking in the Atlantic on April 15, 1912, a memorial tile was added to the frieze in All Saints' Church to record the death of Sidney Conrad Siebert, aged thirty, who perished in the wreck. At the time of the disaster, Mr. Siebert was aboard the 'Titanic' with his brother-in-law, Charles Savage, both of whom were serving as stewards. Mr. Savage was a survivor from the ill-fated vessel and though Mr. Siebert was pulled aboard one of the lifeboats, after swimming for nearly a mile he succumbed from the cold and exhaustion. He was eventually recommitted to the deep from which he had seemed to have escaped. Mr. Siebert was married to Miss Winifred Rose Savage on October 5, 1907, at All Saints' Church. Both young men attended the local National School as boys, a circumstance of which the half-masted school flag was a reminder.

BRIGHTLINGSEA CREEK

CK30

71. Brightlingsea Creek viewed from St. Osyth Stone in 1903/04. The newly-opened Anchor Hotel dominates the local waterside while the ketch 'Fiona' (CK30) and the smacks 'Zouave' (407CK) and 'Irex' (152CK) lie at anchor in the Creek. Captain Arthur Cook's 'Iris' just edges into the picture in the foreground. The 'Fiona' was the last Brightlingsea sailing smack to dredge for scallops 'up Channel'. This was in 1931, and, after being laid-up locally and in Wivenhoe, was handed over to the Sea Scouts in 1947 for use as their guardship. 'Fiona' was moored at Fingrinhoe, near Ballast Quay Farm, where she remained until broken-up twenty years later.

72. The Brightlingsea Deputy's badge and chain was presented by Mr. John Bateman in 1893. The badge is a very fine opal known as 'The Great Opal' which Mr. Bateman had carved to represent a seascape. Round the mount is the Latin inscription 'Urbs Brictriceseiae ex dono Johannis Bateman' (The town of Brightlingsea by the gift of John Bateman). The pendant has the inscription 'Pulchra Matre Filia Pulchrior' (From a beautiful mother, a more beautiful daughter). The chain of solid silver is made of alternate links of oyster shells and crossed sprats. Held in trust by the Corporation of Sandwich, the Deputy's badge and chain is to be the badge of the Mayor in the event of Brightlingsea becoming a Corporation. If the appointment of the Deputy should cease in any other way, it is to return to the head of the Bateman family. The chain was designed by Piers Egerton Warburton, Esq., late MP for Mid-Cheshire and made by Mr. M.G. Chambers, silversmith of Colchester. The badge was carved by Mr. C. Bryant of 33 New Bond Street, London.

73. The staff of W.F. Pattison and Son, sailmakers, shipchandlers and general outfitters, at Brightlingsea's Waterside, pose for the photographer with Mr. William Pattison junior (front, right). Two of the local mariners in the rear rank sport the navy-blue guernseys signifying their membership of the yachts 'Anemone V' and 'Julia', respectively, successful in the 1920's regattas.

74. Brightlingsea's Reading Room in Duke Street and its caretaker, Mr. Frederick Cross. After a preliminary meeting on November 21, 1879, and a further meeting on December 26, 1879, the Rooms were launched. The first premises were above Pannell's stores in Victoria Place and removal to a rented house at No. 1 Duke Street took place two years later. Mr. Cross succeeded Mrs. Pinnick as caretaker in 1896 and served in that capacity until his death at the age of eighty-one in January, 1906. For many years he was skipper of the yawl 'Adelaide'. In 1897 the Room became the gift of the late Mr. James Aldous, the legacy receiving the approval of the Charity Commissioners with Trustees appointed. It wasn't long before the Room became a games centre, then a lending library was added. In 1921 a billiard table was purchased and this attracted both young and older men into membership. By 1937 the local demand for billiards was at an end and the table was sold. A decision to put the billiard room portion of the premises to fuller use resulted in its hire to the Essex County Council for use as a branch of its Public Library from 1938 until the opening of the County Library in New Street in March, 1968. Today the Reading Room is contained in but a single room, once the caretaker's dining room, and this has also taken on the additional role of the local museum.

75. Retired Essex police sergeant, George Every, in addition to his two Waterside shops, and later a restaurant, was the proprietor of the old barge 'Pandora' which he had converted as a sweetshop and tearoom and sited on St. Osyth Stone. Here holidaymakers, during the summer months, could buy sweets, ices, doughnuts and cups of tea and, if they wished, sit at little tables in the barge and eat their purchases. Goods for sale in the barge were kept replenished from the Waterside shops and these were ferried from the Hard to 'Toozey Stone'. Seen in our picture postcard seated outside 'Pandora', in 1910 or thereabouts, are four local 'old worthies'.

HUTS ON ST. OSYTH STONE. BRIGHTLINGSEA.

76. Before the development of the present promenade, in 1923, the only available beach with sand was across the Colne at St. Osyth Stone. Here was sand in plenty and beach huts for hire. There were always ferrymen available at the Hard to 'row you across' on high days and holidays to Brightlingsea's Riviera.